101

Parenting Affirmations

By Kidsstoppress.com

Author's Note

To quote the wise words of **Buddha**: *What we think, we become.*

Think you're destined to fail and you will. But believe you're in charge of your own success and you'll achieve your dreams. Wishful thinking? Maybe not.

Telling yourself how awesome you are can seem bizarre but believe me it works. That is the power of positive affirmations. Positive affirmations work by altering your thoughts. Your thoughts affect your mood and your actions which results in you feeling and acting in different ways.

Let me be clear. You can't use an affirmation like a magic spell. In other words, you can't just say it and expect things to happen. I mean wouldn't we all love to say, "I will be a millionaire tomorrow" and have it happen? Unfortunately, they don't work like that.

Basically, the positive affirmation affects your thoughts which then affects your actions causing you to make positive changes. Sounds right?

#simplifyingparenting

Did you know that the power of positive affirmations is actually backed by neuroscience? So, humans are constantly thinking and that causes signs to be sent to the brain and in the release of neurotransmitters. These chemicals control virtually all of your body's functions, including your mood and feelings. Now, what happens is that when we stay positive and repeat the same things over and over again it activates the reward circuit in your brain and neuroscience studies have shown that via neuroplasticity, your thoughts change your brain, your cells, and even your genes.

For example, when people practice gratitude, they get a surge of rewarding neurotransmitters, like dopamine and norepinephrine, and experience a general uplift of the mind.

I have stopped complaining about life because I understand that every situation is a result of a choice. I have chosen the way we live, the way I am raising my kids, the amount of time I spend on social, the amount I play with my kids, and the amount of importance I give over what people think about me vs what I think about myself. Everything is a choice – and I made it.

We have curated affirmations that are going to boost your self-esteem, motivate you and encourage positive changes in your life.

This book along with others makes for a great present for new parents, a quick read for current parents, or a coffee-table conversation starter.

This book is 1 of 3 in our series of Parenting. The other two are doses of moments when you will need a little pep talk and some humour in your life on days when nothing seems to be going right. Yes, we all have those days. Share your favourite affirmations as you go through the book. We are just a handle away @kidsstoppress and @mansi.zaveri.

We hope you enjoy it as much as we have loved putting it together.

XOXO,
Mansi Zaveri

#simplifyingparenting

Your Handy Guide To Start Writing Affirmations

When you start writing affirmations you should keep a few things in mind. Take a moment to read through these steps and you'll be writing positive affirmations that are supercharged in no time at all!

Let's start with the basics...

The simplest way to start writing affirmations is to write a series of "I am" statements that describe what you want to have or experience.

"I am happy"

"I am wealthy"

Simple enough isn't it?

Write your affirmations as an expression of "grateful having", rather than wanting or needing.

See this

"I am so happy and grateful for my wonderful new house!"

You can also begin your affirmations with words such as:

"I know..."

"I have..."

"I love..."

...or any other positive, affirmative statement.

When you write your affirmations, write them in the present tense. Write as though you are experiencing what you desire right now.

Put yourself in the frame of mind of already having what you want, and then let the universe figure out the most efficient and harmonious way to bring it to you.

101
Parenting
Affirmations

By Kidsstoppress.com

1

I am a great mom. Great moms
also have bad days.

———

2

I am beautiful with all the scars.
I have brought life into this world
and that is a miracle in itself.

3

I am a confident woman.
My children look up to me
every day.

———

4

I am a blessing to my family.

———

5

My children are lucky to have such a warm, caring and loving mother.

———

6

I am worthy of having such
beautiful children.

———

#simplifyingparenting

7

I am courageous. I can share
my vulnerabilities with my child.
They need a mother, not a
superwoman though I can be that
also on some days.

———

#kspaffi

rmations

8

I release myself of being or showing that we are a perfect family. We are a good healthy, loving and caring family.

———

9

We are blessed to be together.

______

10

My children love me unconditionally.

———

11

I always need to demonstrate the love, actions and courage that I expect from my children.

———

12

I am blessed to be a parent.

______

13

I release expectations to enjoy
and live in the present moment.

———

14

Moments with my children
can be fun, unstructured and
unproductive.

———

15

When I am at work, I am providing
for my kids and family, to give
them the best life I can.

———

#simplifyingparenting

16

When I go on a date night with my husband, I am teaching my kids that relationships are built by investing time, energy and love in them.

———

17

When I leave my kids behind sometimes, they learn to be independent in the care of people I trust.

———

#simplifyingparenting

18

When I feel overwhelmed, I just need to remember I am bigger than the problem.

———

19

When the 100 parent compartments open up in my brain all I need to do is remind myself I have boundless energy.

———

20

I forgive my children's flaws.
Forgiveness is the key to
happiness.

———

21

I choose joy today.

———

22

Today I will make mundane tasks fun for us as a family.

———

23

I am open to learning with my children again.

———

24

Today I will drop the cape and the pressures of being a super mom or a super dad. I just want to be a good parent.

———

25

I am a good parent even if I have forgotten to send something to school, been late for a pick-up, or missed a deadline or a birthday party.

———

26

I am proud of a body that housed
a life. It needs love, care and so
much respect.

———

27

All that I need to be a good parent is within me.

———

#positive

parenting

28

My children don't need a perfect parent. They want someone who loves them, can play with them and hold their hand no matter what.

———

29

When my children don't share it
does not mean they don't love
me. It only means I need to walk a
little closer to their hearts.

———

30

When my child hurts me, I am still a good mom with a child who is having a hard day.

———

31

I will not bucket or label my kids. They are meant for jars, not creative humans.

———

32

I am indifferent to the decisions
made by other moms.

————

33

My child's performance is not a report card of my parenting skills.

———

34

My child is an individual who is fully capable of creating their own life. We are different.

———

35

I can handle all the parenting situations that life poses for me. I will let intuition and love guide me.

____

I am teaching my kids to be afraid of nothing.

———

37

On some days I need to accept, things will be over the place. It's just a day. It will pass.

———

38

I am more than a parent. My children, family and friends all appreciate that about me.

———

It is okay to say no.
It's not a bad word.

———

#self

love

40

It's okay to ask for help.
It's not a sign of weakness.

———

41

Spending time away from my kids is also a sign of being a good parent.

———

#simplifyingparenting

42

Different families have different rules. I am making a rule book that is open for change, and dialogue and works for my family.

———

43

My messy bun, mom jeans and
leggings are just a few "Wow!"
things my kids love about me.

———

I will kiss my kids goodnight in person or over a call on most days fully aware that they won't be little anymore and that the sun should never set on an argument.

———

45

Saying sorry to my kids is a sign of strength and equality.

———

46

Today I will let go of what the world thinks of me as a parent.

———

47

Being frustrated doesn't make me a bad mom.

———

48

I cannot control how I feel, but I can control how I act.

———

49

It's okay to wonder how things could be.

———

50

I am going to find joy in the little wins.

———

51

I cannot control the future.

———

#itsokayto

notbeokay

52

It's ok. This is the recovery time
for me and my child.

———

It's ok that I need to rest
more than I thought I
would need to.

———

54

I am a warrior mom. My body is stronger than it has ever been before.

———

$$55$$

I am vibrant. And I am beautiful.

———

56

I am going to allow my body to heal and be stronger.

———

57

I am not alone in this journey.

———

It's ok that I need time to be by myself.

————

59

I embrace my body. I love the new me.

______

60

I am good enough in all that I do.

____

61

It's ok to cry at the drop of a hat.
Even the strong cry.

———

62

I matter. Even on days where I
feel invisible.

———

63

I am worthy of good things.

————

#you

matter

64

I am strong. Even if I have
meltdowns.

______

65

I am not a pushover. My presence is valuable.

———

66

I love myself for all that I am and all that I do.

———

67

I am happy the way I am raising
my children.

————

68

I forgive myself for my failures. I
am human too.

———

69

I will make sure not to control
my family.

———

70

I'll be my original self. I don't need
to prove myself to anyone.

———

71

It's okay to cry. I have a right to express myself too.

———

72

It's okay if I am feeling lost today. I will figure it out tomorrow. It's not over.

———

73

It's okay that I want to love myself
more. I deserve this love.

———

It's okay that I am not the best version of myself.

———

75

Thankful for the real ones in my life. That's all it takes to raise a happy family.

———

76

I deserve it all. I am working hard
on it every day.

———

I am resting and pampering
myself. It is part of my growth.

———

78

I will treat my soul with kindness,
care and empathy.

———

79

There's noting wrong in taking quiet bathroom breaks.

______

#blessedto

beaparent

80

A full 8-hour sleep. The love. The appreciation. The friends. The support. A life where I eat what I like. I deserve all this.

———

81

I believe in myself. I always will no matter what.

———

82

My growth is a continuous process.

———

83

My job at home is worth a million.

———

84

I am enough. Nothing more and nothing less.

______

I listen to my heart and do what is best for my family and me.

———

There is peace and love in my house, even in the middle of chaos.

———

87

Taking care of myself is also an
important responsibility.

———

88

It's ok to not have it together always and it's okay to ask for help.

———

89

I am a goddess. The bearer of life. The glue of the family. I am so much more than what I give myself credit for.

90

It's okay for me not to have solutions to every problem.

———

91

I can be wrong sometimes. It's what makes me human.

———

92

I am not invisible. I will block
some time for myself!

———

93

My health and well-being matter too, as much as everybody else.

———

I will take care of myself so I can take care of those who I love.

————

95

It is necessary to take out time for myself.

———————

96

I am never in a rush; my timing is perfect.

———

97

I don't need to be a "perfect" parent. My children love me with my flaws.

———

I am doing a great job with the
tools that are available to me.

———

99

I will take each day as it comes, and not try to tick mark everything on my to-do list!

———

100

I am the best for my family and I am making them so very proud by doing what I do and by just being me.

———

101

I fall in love with myself every day.
I am such a magnificent being.

———

#Thanks

Some of these affirmations are inspired from fellow moms and most are from our real-life experiences.

We thank all parents for sharing their thoughts with the world.

Disclaimer: In case we missed giving you credit, it was not intentional. We were unable to find the sources of some of our favourite quotes.

Tap into your emotions and pen down the
affirmations that are close to your heart here.

#simplifyingparenting

Tap into your emotions and pen down the
affirmations that are close to your heart here.

Tap into your emotions and pen down the
affirmations that are close to your heart here.

Team Credit

Telling yourself how awesome you are can seem bizarre but believe me it works. That is the power of positive affirmations. We have curated affirmations that are going to boost your self-esteem, motivate you and encourage positive changes in your life.

We would like to thank all those who have worked extremely hard to make the 101 Positive Parenting Affirmations book possible.

Mansi Zaveri for her drive, vision and passion. She's been the mentor we needed to drive this through. Without her unconditional support and constant encouragement this book would not have been possible.

Parul Gupta for being the steady anchor we always need for projects like this. As a teen parent she needs a lot of laughter & tons of positive energy and through this book she's helped bring it to you too.

Tanya Lemos for her patience, the constant follow ups and for all the never-ending changes we have been making to make this book perfect for you. Her calm and composure has been a great help in making sure this book delivered all that we promised.